Bats, Cats, and Rats

by Dave Miller, Ph.D.

A.P. "Learn to Read" Series

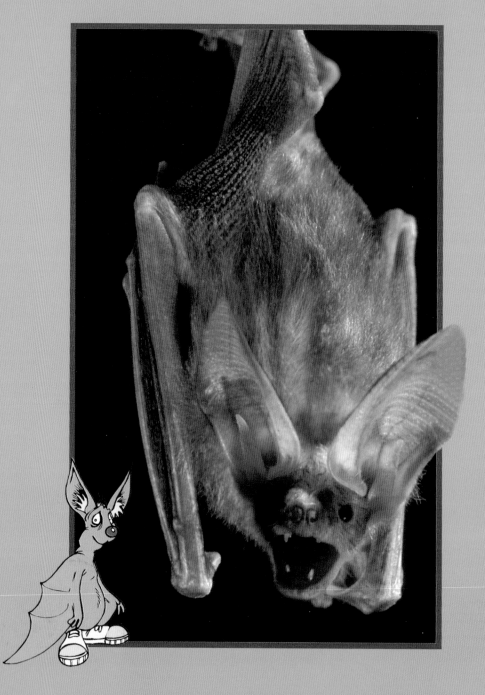

God made bats.

God did that.

Bats fly.

Bats fly
up, up, up.

Bats fly fast.

God made bats.

God made cats.

God
made big cats.

God made small cats

God made fat cats.

Cats are soft.

Cats purr.

Cats do not

put on hats.

God made cats.

God made rats.

See the rat?

That rat is fat.

Rats can bite!

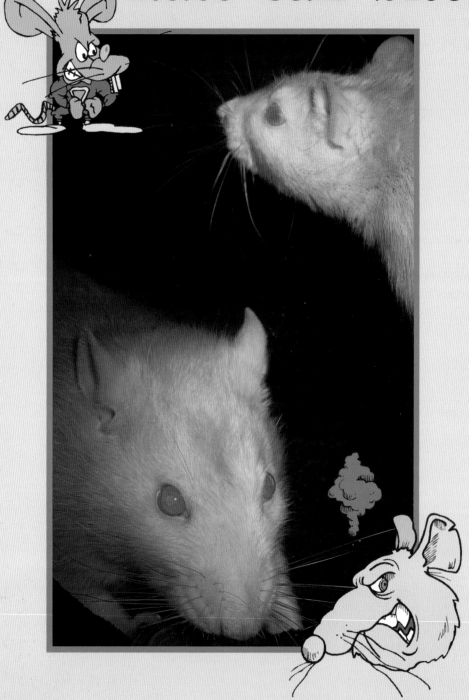

Do not go to rats!

Cats can eat rats.

A rat has a
long tail.

God made rats.

God made bats, cats, and rats.

God made them all.

God made them all
on days five and six.

God is good!

The "Learn to Read" Series:
A Word to Parents

Rationale: To provide books for children (ages 3-6) from Christian homes for the purpose of assisting them in **learning to read** while simultaneously introducing them to the **Creator** and His **creation.**

Difficulty Level

The following listing provides a breakdown of the number and length of words in *Bats, Cats, and Rats* (not counting plurals and duplicates):

Total Number of Words: 40

1 - One Letter Word

a

6 - Two letter words

up, do, on, is, go, to

21 - Three letter words

God, bat, did, fly, cat, big, fat,

are, not, put, hat, rat, see, the,

can, eat, has, and, all, day, six

11 - Four letter words

made, that, fast, soft, purr

bite, long, tail, them, good, five

1 - Five Letter Word

small

Drawings by
Kyrsti Dubcak, Age 7

The A.P. Reader Series

LEVEL 1 **"Learn to Read"**

1. *Dogs, Frogs, and Hogs*
2. *Bats, Cats, and Rats*
3. *Birds, Bugs, and Bees*

LEVEL 2 **"Early Reader"**

1. *God Made the World*
2. *God Made Dinosaurs*
3. *God Made Animals*
4. *God Made Insects*
5. *God Made Plants*
6. *God Made Fish*

LEVEL 3 **"Advanced Reader"**

Coming Soon!

We are continuing to expand the number of titles in each series. Be sure to check our Web site for our newest books.
www.ApologeticsPress.org